Gifted or Goof Off?
Fact & Fiction
of the Famous

by Nancy Polette
Caricatures by John Steele

Pieces of
Learning

© 2004 Nancy Polette
CLC0304
ISBN 1-931334-23-4
www.piecesoflearning.com
Printed in the U.S.A.

Table of Contents

FACT OR FICTION?

HANS CHRISTIAN ANDERSEN
COULDN'T SPELL

HANS CHRISTIAN ANDERSEN
1805-1875

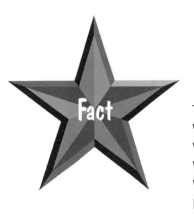

Fact

Take one very lonely little boy
Who was funny to look at
Who daydreamed through lessons
Who missed more school than he attended
Who never learned to spell
But who loved fantasy tales and you have
Hans Christian Andersen,
One of the world's greatest storytellers.

Growing up in Denmark was not easy for this strange-looking little boy. He was tall and skinny and had a funny-looking nose, a perfect target for bullies. Just like *The Ugly Duckling,* he was picked on because he was different.

To escape the real world Hans became a daydreamer and paid little attention to classes. While he was an excellent reader, his spelling skills left a lot to be desired.

When he could no longer face the bullies, Hans would skip school and spend his time at the wharves watching the ships come in and listening to the tales of the old fishwives as they talked together cleaning fish or mending nets. The tales were of magical creatures and strange happenings. The young boy listened and dreamed of writing stories like

© Steele

that. He escaped the real world by making up stories in his head. *The Ugly Duckling* is, in fact, the story of Andersen's life. It is the tale of a creature rejected by the world because of its ugliness, but who, in later life is accepted for its beauty.

Andersen, the boy who never learned to spell, was later in life to tell his stories to kings and queens and finally, to the whole world. And the world listened to these magical tales then as it still does today.

FACT OR FICTION?

ROALD DAHL'S TEACHERS URGED HIM TO BECOME A WRITER

ROALD DAHL
1916-1990

Fiction

"I have never met anybody who so persistently writes the exact opposite of what he means. He seems incapable of marshaling his thoughts on paper."

This was the complaint of one of Roald Dahl's teachers who probably predicted that the boy would never write anything that made sense.

The author of *Charlie and the Chocolate Factory, Matilda, The BFG* and dozens of other books for children and adults really hated school. At Repton, a school for boys, he watched helplessly as younger boys were beaten by masters and older students. He especially disliked the matron, who ruled the place where the boys slept, and he re-creates her for others to see in *Matilda*, where the head of "Crunchem Hall," Miss Trunchbull, throws students out the window.

Because Roald was always so much bigger than those around him, he knew what it was like to be different and to live in a world made for smaller people. When he wrote *The BFG* (The Big Friendly Giant) he was probably writing about himself.

This boy who hated school loved adventure. He traveled to the diamond mines of Africa. He flew a fighter plane in World War II and was

© Steele

badly injured when his plane crashed. About his injuries he said, "You do get bits of magic from enormous bumps on the head."

Was it the "bumps on the head" that gave him a special magic to write for children? His early teachers would say that the "bumps" finally helped him to get his thoughts in order. What do you think?

FACT OR FICTION?

1st Prize
Writing

© Steele

**CHARLES DICKENS WON
THE WRITING PRIZE IN
GRAMMAR SCHOOL**

CHARLES DICKENS
1812-1870

Fiction

The year is 1818. The place is London, England. It is bedtime. The Dickens children are gathered around the storyteller who claws the air with both hands and utters a long, low hollow groan. "And then," she said, "Captain Murderer made pies out of his wives."

Six-year-old Charles Dickens was terrified at the stories told to him by Mary Weller, the nursemaid. At the same time, he longed to hear the stories again (which she said were quite true) but Mary was let go because the Dickens family had no money to pay her.

Charles loved reading stories and making up stories in his head, but no grammar prizes were waiting for the boy at school. In fact, when he was twelve years old, there was no school. His father's salary as a clerk was not enough to take care of such a large family. They sent Charles' father to prison because he could not pay money he owed. Charles had to go to work to support the family. He obtained a job in a dye factory putting black labels on bottles. At the end of each fourteen-hour day he was black from head to foot. He hated the job, he hated the black ink, he hated the long hours.

Day after day while pasting labels on the bottles, Charles dreamed of escaping the awful place. Perhaps some long lost wealthy relative

© Steele

would leave him a great sum of money. He did not have a long lost wealthy relative, but the dream helped to make the awful job bearable. Years later those dreams helped Charles Dickens to become one of England's most popular authors. One novel, *Oliver Twist*, tells the story of a young boy who has to make a living the best way he can. A cruel man teaches him to steal what he needs. Do you suppose Dickens was writing about himself or was this another dream?

FACT OR FICTION?

Let me guess.
My book has
been turned
down again.

© Steele

TWENTY-SEVEN PUBLISHERS TURNED DOWN DR. SEUSS'S FIRST BOOK

11

DR. SEUSS
1904-1991

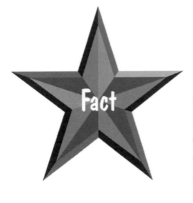

Fact

Theodore was excited any time he got to visit his father's workplace. His father was curator of the Forest Park Zoo. He not only wanted to see the animals, he wanted to draw the animals. He drew animals on tablets, in notebooks, on paper napkins and tablecloths. He drew animals anywhere and everywhere he could. In school he probably drew animals to decorate his homework.

When Theodore graduated from Dartmouth College in 1925 he found there were no jobs for people who liked to draw animals. He sent his cartoon drawings to many magazines. One of his cartoons caught the attention of an advertising man at Standard Oil. He hired Theodore to draw cartoon ads for their insecticide, *Flit*. People liked the cartoons that usually featured a monster-like creature attacking a family. Then someone would cry out, "Quick, Henry, the *Flit*!"

Twelve years later on a ship bound for Europe, Theodore had an idea for a children's book. He wrote *To Think I Saw It on Mulberry Street* and sent the manuscript to twenty-seven different publishers. Each time it was rejected. But Theodore was not discouraged. He convinced a friend in the publishing business to take a chance on the book and it was published.

Dr. Seuss is best known for his book *Cat In the Hat,* which he wrote as a fun easy reader for children just learning to read. He wrote *Green Eggs and Ham* on a bet with a fellow author who told him writing a whole book using just fifty words

was impossible. If you count, you will see there are only fifty words in *Green Eggs and Ham*.

During World War II, Dr. Seuss joined the army and became Captain Geisel. They sent him to Hollywood where he used his talents in creating documentaries as part of the Signal Corps Unit. He not only won many awards for his work, but received the Legion of Merit from his grateful country as well. After the war he continued to write for grateful children who at last found fun books that they could read.

FACT OR FICTION?

LUCILLE BALL'S DRAMA SCHOOL TEACHER
TOLD HER SHE HAD NO TALENT

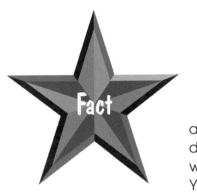

Fact

Lucille Ball had always dreamed of being an actress. She was so anxious to realize her dream that she dropped out of high school when she was fifteen years old and went to New York City. There she became a student at the John Murray Anderson Drama School. She worked hard, but her instructors told her to go home. She had no talent.

Lucille did not go home. Every time any New York theatre posted an audition notice, Lucille was there. She had hoped to become part of a Broadway chorus line but was turned away again and again.

It was then that Lucille became a model. Hollywood producers saw some of her photographs. She went to Hollywood and got her wish to be a chorus girl in her first film, *Roman Scandals*, in 1934. For the next sixteen years Lucille Ball appeared in more than forty films. In one of these films, *Too Many Girls*, she fell in love with another actor. His name was Desi Arnaz, and he and Lucille were married. They had two children, a son and a daughter.

While she was making movies, Lucille also starred as a zany wife in the radio series *My Favorite Husband.* When CBS asked her to play the same role in a television series, she said yes, but only if Desi could play the part of her husband. The show was re-titled *I Love Lucy,* and Lucille Ball became a super star.

The girl whom they sent home from acting school showed her instructors that almost any dream can come true with talent, hard work and determination.

FACT OR FICTION?

I can't believe I got an "A."

JIM CARREY WAS AN "A" STUDENT

JIM CARREY
1962-

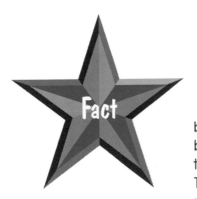

Fact

As his fans might guess, Jim Carrey was a boy with a wild imagination, a body that would bend like a rubber band, and more energy than two youths his age. At Blessed Trinity School in Toronto fellow students laughed at his comic routines. But the gifted clown was equally good at his studies since his grades were often straight "A's".

Jim Carrey's bright mind and comic wit meant success in any profession. He had only to choose. But the choice was taken from him at age fourteen. Jim's father lost his job, and hard times were ahead. The family moved to another town where Jim had to take a factory job. He tried to continue high school while working eight-hour shifts. His grades dropped. High school classes were the only time he had to sleep.

Jim dropped out of high school, and with the help of his parents, began performing at comedy clubs. Did he become an instant hit? No! His first attempts with an audience met boos rather than laughter.

Jim was not ready to quit. He moved to Los Angeles and managed to land a spot at the Comedy Store. The pay was low, but the exposure was high. He caught the eye of comic greats of the day. Rodney Dangerfield and David Letterman gave him spots on their shows. Movie offers followed. His starring role in *Ace Ventura* made him a hit with fans and led to more

I can't believe I got an "A."

© Steele

and more movie roles including *The Mask, Dumb and Dumber, How the Grinch Stole Christmas, The Majestic,* and *Bruce Almighty.*

Jim Carrey, like many others, knew childhood poverty, hard work and disappointment. Suppose he had given up his dream of becoming a comedian? They say that laughter is healthy. Think how many laughs the world would have missed.

FACT OR FICTION?

I thought my records were great.

© Steele

CHER'S FIRST RECORDS WERE FLOPS

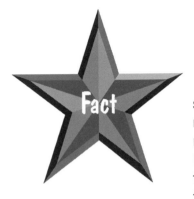

The lanky teenager with the fly-away hair stood before the microphone. Engineers in the recording studio twisted knobs and dials. The musicians tuned up. It was to be Bonnie Jo Mason's big break, her first solo recording! When the record was released Bonnie Jo waited for the success that was to be hers. The recording was a big flop. Only later would the singer drop the stage name, Bonnie Jo, and become Cher. Her birth name is Cherilyn Sarkisin.

How did Cher become a household name? No one really knows. She wasn't blond and blue-eyed like other popular singers. She was not petite. Her long dark hair was as untamed as a lion's mane. Her clothes were outrageous and to many, shocking.

Cher was born in 1946 to a childhood of poverty. At age sixteen she dropped out of high school and met Sonny Bono, a songwriter. It was Sonny who arranged for that first recording session. He knew that Cher had a special talent but had a hard time convincing others. It was when the two recorded a song together that Cher's singing career took off. The two began to receive offers as *Sonny and Cher* and made one hit record after another.

In the 70's the *Sonny and Cher Show* was a television hit, and in 1975 Cher had her own television series. A major role in a Broadway play led to

movie offers and Cher showed her talent as an actress in both *Silkwood* and *Mask* and won an Academy Award for *Moonstruck*.

Cher's talent and enduring qualities have made her a star for nearly 40 years. A childhood of poverty, a high school dropout, early recording failures and other disappointments all served as fuel for her determination to succeed . . . and she did!

FACT OR FICTION?

TOM CRUISE WAS A
STRUGGLING READER

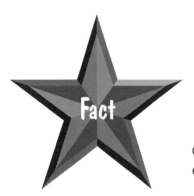

TOM CRUISE
1962-

As a young boy, the world was not Tom Cruise's oyster. In fact, it was more like a vulture, eating up his hopes and dreams.

Mix together a father who kept moving his family from town to town, a family that often wondered where the next dollar would come from, a young boy with severe reading problems, and you have a recipe for failure.

Tom did not fail, despite the handicaps. He was outstanding in athletics that helped him to fit in at each of the twelve schools he attended. For a time he thought he might make it as a professional wrestler, but a knee injury brought a halt to that dream.

The quality that best defines Tom Cruise from childhood to adulthood is determination. After playing leading parts in high school productions of *Godspell* and *Guys and Dolls*, Tom decided that acting was his future and he headed to New York where they turned him down in audition after audition. He met the same fate in California but his determination paid off. He landed bit parts until his appearance in *Taps* got the attention of other producers. His acting career took off with the starring role in Ann Rice's *Interview With the Vampire*. Is he still a struggling reader? Yes. He learns his lines by having them taped for him.

Today Tom Cruise is a major star. His films have earned more than one billion dollars with many more to come. There were many times in his early life when he had to abandon one dream for another, but determination paid off as he met each challenge, seeing every obstacle as an opportunity to grow not only as an actor but as a person.

FACT OR FICTION?

I thought my cartoons were really good.

WALT DISNEY'S CARTOONS WERE REJECTED BY THE CHICAGO TRIBUNE

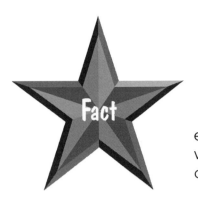

Fact

The young man gave his cartoons to the editor. He waited for the answer. If the answer was "YES," Walt would be a newspaper cartoonist. The answer was "NO!"

The closest Walt Disney came to working for a newspaper was as a delivery boy. Walt was nine when his father's farm failed and the family moved to Kansas City. Walt's father bought a newspaper route and nine-year-old Walt and his brother delivered the papers seven days a week in temperatures ranging from ten below zero to 110 in the sun. There was no sleeping late. There was no customer to be skipped . . . and there was little time for the cartooning that Walt loved so much.

The newspaper routes ended seven years later. Walt was sixteen when the family moved to Chicago. He finished high school there and took cartooning classes at night. But again, he had to put his cartooning on hold. In 1918 the world was on fire. War was tearing up most of Europe. Walt set aside his dreams of cartooning and tried to join the army. He was too young.

Not to be stopped at something he was determined to do, Walt joined the Red Cross, and they sent him overseas as an ambulance driver.

I thought my cartoons were really good.

© Steele

When the war ended, Walt returned home and started his own company. He was twenty-one years old. The company ran out of money, and Walt headed for Hollywood. There, in 1927, he created the cartoon character that helped him achieve his dream.

Millions of fans should be grateful that the *Chicago Tribune* turned down Walt's cartoons. If Walt had spent his life as a newspaper man, Mickey Mouse might never have been created!

FACT OR FICTION?

Go ahead, fire me
and make my day!

© Steele

CLINT EASTWOOD WAS FIRED BY
UNIVERSAL STUDIOS BECAUSE
HE COULDN'T ACT

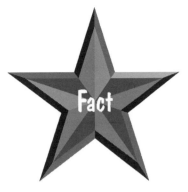

Fact

CLINT EASTWOOD
1930-

No one who knew Clint Eastwood as a young bit player at Universal Studios would have predicted super stardom for him. Born in 1930 at the beginning of the Great Depression, Clint moved with his family from city to city as his father searched for work. He attended ten different schools during his elementary school years and was never in one school long enough to form close friendships. Perhaps this is the reason he is known as a loner, very much like the characters he plays on screen.

Sometimes when his father was away looking for work, Clint and his mother would stay at his grandfather's farm where he learned to ride horses. Though the family moved around a great deal, it was a loving family from whom Clint learned good values.

After high school Clint took numerous outdoor jobs from cutting lumber to digging swimming pools. He also enrolled in college and was thinking about getting a degree in business when friends urged him to try acting. They hired him at Universal Studios and gave him small parts in the horror films *The Revenge of the Creature* and *Tarantula*. A small part in *Never Say Goodbye* was his last at Universal. They fired him and told him he couldn't act and that his "adam's apple" was too big.

Go ahead, fire me and make my day!

© Steele

Clint was about to go back to digging swimming pools when he got a part in the TV series *Rawhide*. Clint stayed with the series seven years, then rose to stardom in "spaghetti westerns" including *A Fistful of Dollars*. The westerns were followed by the "Dirty Harry" films that were equally popular. The man who couldn't act had proven his critics wrong.

FACT OR FICTION?

HARRISON FORD PERFORMS
REAL LIFE RESCUES

© Nancy Polette

HARRISON FORD
1942-

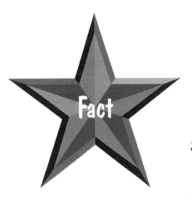

Fact

He saved Princess Leah from Darth Vader in *Star Wars*.

He saved all those aboard *Air Force One*.

He performed countless rescues as *Indiana Jones*.

His name is Harrison Ford, and in real life he is Commander of his own air force!

He keeps four planes and a helicopter at the retreat where he lives near Jackson, Wyoming. He is a licensed pilot who really does perform real-life rescues.

In August of 2000, two women set out for a long hike up Table Mountain. High mountains have thinner air and less oxygen than lower altitudes. Nearing the top of the mountain, one of the women was struck with altitude sickness and collapsed. There was no way she could make it back down the mountain. The nearest help was five miles away.

Luckily, another hiker had a cell phone and called 911. The local sheriff''s department contacted Ford who is a volunteer with the Mountain Rescuers. He answered the call at once and within minutes his helicopter was in the air heading toward the mountain and the stricken woman.

Does anybody need help?

© Steele

The woman's friend and the hiker managed to get her to a meadow where Ford's helicopter was able to land. With Ford's help she was placed aboard the helicopter and taken to safety.

When he isn't rescuing the world on the silver screen, Harrison Ford continues to be on call from the Sheriff's Department as a Mountain Rescue Volunteer.

FACT OR FICTION?

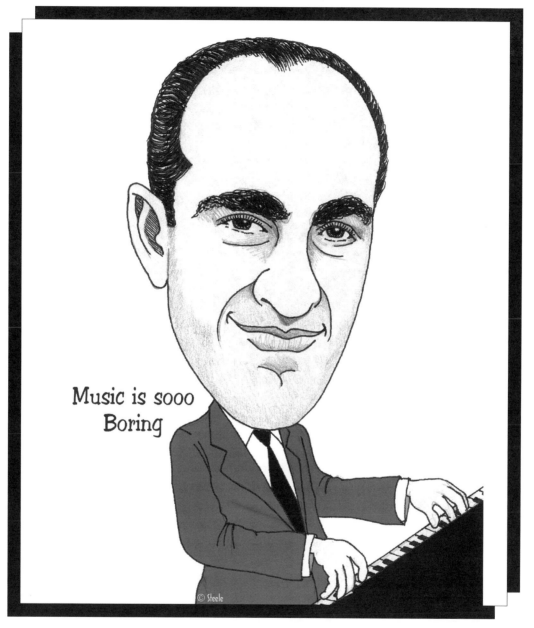

GEORGE GERSHWIN HATED MUSIC

GEORGE GERSHWIN
1898-1937

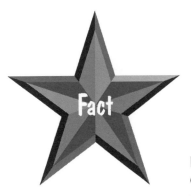

Fact

As a boy George Gershwin hated music but loved a good fight.

You had to be tough to survive on the New York City streets in 1910. The street where George Gershwin lived was in one of the poorest parts of the city. His parents were Russian immigrants who worked hard to keep their family of six together.

As a twelve-year-old, George thought piano playing was for sissies. "Hands are for fighting," he shouted, and his hands were involved in fights almost daily.

Then George met Maxie. Maxie played the violin. It was a sound like no other George had ever heard. It fascinated him. How did Maxie know what notes to play? Who wrote that music? He had to know how such music came to be.

About the same time, George's father bought a used piano for Ira, his brother. George made that piano his! He wanted lessons. He practiced every spare minute. Within two years they were paying him to play the piano at a resort in the Catskill Mountains.

By the time George was seventeen he was composing and selling his own songs. George wrote the music and Ira wrote the words. The songwriters were a huge success. When their songs were used in the movies, the whole country began singing them.

Music is sooo Boring

© Steele

George was not satisfied. He had always wanted to create a kind of music that had never before been played or heard. When he was twenty-six, he achieved his dream. A symphony orchestra performed *Rhapsody in Blue*, and the world came to know a truly original composer. Wouldn't you like to hear it?

FACT OR FICTION?

Next!

WHOOPI GOLDBERG WAS A MAKE-UP ARTIST IN A FUNERAL HOME

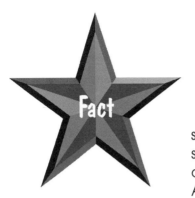

WHOOPI GOLDBERG
1955-

Fact

When Whoopi Goldberg's face shines from the silver screen, what do you see? There is laughter and humor, sadness and compassion, courage and intelligence. All of these qualities were hard won for the little girl who grew up without a father in the mean streets of New York City.

Though she was very bright, Whoopi, whose real name is Caryn Johnson, saw no reason to stay in school. She dropped out of high school in the ninth grade. For several years she did drugs until she realized there was no future for her if she continued down that path. She entered a drug treatment center and won her fight over addiction.

Determined to become an actress, Whoopi Goldberg had to support herself while making her dream come true. At age twenty-five she went to California and joined a group of comedy actors. While this gave her a chance to perform, there was little or no pay. In order to eat she did everything from laying bricks to doing hair and makeup for corpses at a funeral home.

In the early 1980's Whoopi performed wherever there was an audience. A producer saw her on stage and arranged an evening on Broadway for her. This led to her first movie, *The Color Purple,* for which she earned several awards. Many films followed establishing Whoopi Goldberg as a major star.

She has not, however, forgotten her beginnings. She is a major spokesperson for the war on drugs. Her message to young people is simple. "Drugs are not the answer. The road to success lies within yourself."

FACT OR FICTION?

**JAMES EARL JONES WON
THE FIFTH GRADE SPEECH CONTEST**

© Nancy Polette

JAMES EARL JONES
1931-

Young theatergoers shiver with fear when the deep, booming voice cuts across the screen. They know that in the next second the evil Darth Vader will appear and that Luke Skywalker is in big trouble. The deep voice that fills the smallest corners of any room belongs to James Earl Jones. It is probably one of the most recognized voices in the world today. Isn't it amazing that as a child, James Earl Jones seldom spoke at all. He certainly did not win any speech contests.

James Earl Jones was a stutterer. As a child the speech problem was so severe that he became mute, refusing to speak at all for many years. Born Todd Jones in 1931, the boy did not meet his actor father until he was a young man. His grandparents raised him on their farm in Michigan.

In high school the silent boy wrote poetry. One of his teachers asked him to read some of the poems to the class. To the boy's amazement, he was able to read all of the poems without stuttering. Reading and writing poetry unlocked all those years of silence.

After high school James Earl decided to become a doctor. However, he continued speech lessons to completely rid himself of the stutter. It was at this time that friends encouraged him to try an acting career. After a time in the military, James Earl studied acting in New York and starred in the Broadway play *The Great White Hope* for which he received a Tony Award. This success led to parts on the stage, screen and television.

Oooh, I'm Really Good!

© Steele

While their parents shiver at the deep menacing tones of Darth Vader, children today delight in hearing this marvelous voice as Mufasa in *The Lion King*, the voice that almost wasn't heard when James Earl was a child.

FACT OR FICTION?

© Steele

MICHAEL JORDAN WAS CUT FROM
HIS HIGH SCHOOL VARSITY TEAM

MICHAEL JORDAN
1963-

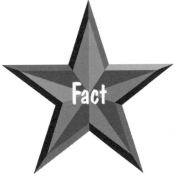

The word was out at Laney High School! They had just posted the basketball varsity team roster. The boys pushed each other aside in the rush to make it to the locker room first. Making the varsity team was tough for a sophomore, but Michael Jordan had high hopes. At six feet nine inches he could see over the heads of most of the boys. His eyes went up and down the list. His name wasn't there. He hadn't made the team.

Michael stared at the list. He saw one name he knew wasn't as good a player as he was. Inside he felt angry. But while the anger didn't show, determination did. Throughout his professional career, Michael thought about that list when the going got tough. "Whenever I was working out and got tired and figured I ought to stop," Michael said, "I'd close my eyes and see that list in the locker room without my name on it, and that usually got me going again."

Michael did make the varsity team as a junior and was the star of the team the next year. His athletic ability earned him a college scholarship.

Michael was the star of the team at the University of North Carolina. In 1984 and 1992 he led the United States basketball team to a gold medal at the Olympics. He joined the Chicago Bulls before finishing college where his acrobatic shots earned him the nickname "Air." The tall, skinny rookie quickly proved himself by leading the Bulls to three World Championships.

© Steele

Michael retired from basketball at the end of the 1993-94 season and tried his hand at baseball. His baseball career lasted one year and he returned to the game he loved in 1995. The next year he led the Bulls to their fourth World Championship. In 1999, at age thirty-five, he retired from the game leaving an impressive record of wins. The boy whose name wasn't even at the bottom of that locker room list, used that first failure as a stepping stone to success. How did he do it? With hard work, determination and dignity.

FACT OR FICTION?

I gotta "C" and I'm all shook up.

© Steele

ELVIS PRESLEY'S HIGH SCHOOL MUSIC TEACHER TOLD HIM HE COULDN'T SING

ELVIS PRESLEY
1935-1977

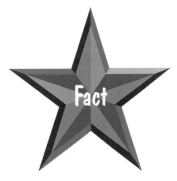

Fact

It is true that Elvis Presley earned a "C" in music at L.C. Hume High School. When his music teacher told him he couldn't sing, he disagreed with her. He told her she just didn't appreciate his kind of music. The next day he brought his guitar to school. When she heard his music, which was a blend of blues and jazz, she told him he was right! She didn't like his kind of music.

Elvis knew a childhood of poverty. They sent his father to prison when the boy was three. Elvis and his mother moved in with his father's parents who had little to share. In 1948, when Elvis was thirteen, the family moved to Memphis where he attended high school.

After high school the boy who couldn't sing worked as a machinist and as a truck driver, but singing was what he had to do. He haunted clubs and radio stations. Elvis was rarely found without his guitar. He sang wherever and whenever he could. His dream was to make a record, and he was often found on the steps of Memphis recording studios. Whether owners of recording studios were tired of seeing him or whether they thought he had talent, he finally got his chance. He recorded his first two songs for Sun Records in 1954. Two years later he had his first hit record, Heartbreak Hotel. Appearances on the Ed Sullivan Show rocked the young singer to fame. Hollywood beckoned, and he made the first of thirty-three movies, Love Me Tender, in 1956.

I gotta "C"
and I'm
all shook up.

© Steele

Elvis's career was interrupted when he served two years in the army. After his discharge he married and had one daughter. He gave generous gifts to friends and relatives, perhaps making up for the years of being poor. He liked to have people around him and people loved him for his humility and kindness to others.

The young man who "couldn't sing" went on to sell more than one billion records. Some of his recordings continue to hit the top of the charts more than twenty-five years after his death.

FACT OR FICTION?

Film School
Dropout

© Steele

STEVEN SPIELBERG WAS REJECTED FROM FILM MAKING SCHOOL

© Nancy Polette

STEVEN SPIELBERG
1946-

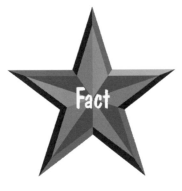

Imagine a little boy who loved to dream. When the teacher was explaining multiplication, the little boy dreamed of the puppet shows he would put on after school. Picture a little boy who loved to draw. When the teacher was explaining nouns and verbs, he drew stages and characters.

That little boy was Steven Spielberg, one of the most respected and important film makers of all time. Yet, because he was a dreamer and a drawer and didn't pay attention in school, his grades were not very good. His dreaming carried through high school, and when he applied for admission to study film making at the University of California, they rejected him.

As a child Steven spent much time alone. His family moved frequently so making friends was hard. To make his dreams come true, Steven made his first movie when he was twelve. It was a three-minute cowboy movie. At age seventeen he made a two and one-half hour film titled *Firelight*. He wanted people to see his film in a real theatre. He was able to talk a friend at a Phoenix theatre into showing it one time.

While Steven did not get into the University of California, he did enroll in college and while there directed a short film. Universal Studios

purchased the film, and they hired Steven to direct television shows. It wasn't long before the young director showed that he could do a lot more than dream. His creative work on *Night Gallery, Columbo* and other TV shows brought offers to direct full length films including *Sugarland Express, Jaws, Star Wars,* the *Indiana Jones* films and many more.

Through his extraordinary films, the dreamer had finally found a way to share his dreams with the world.

FACT OR FICTION?

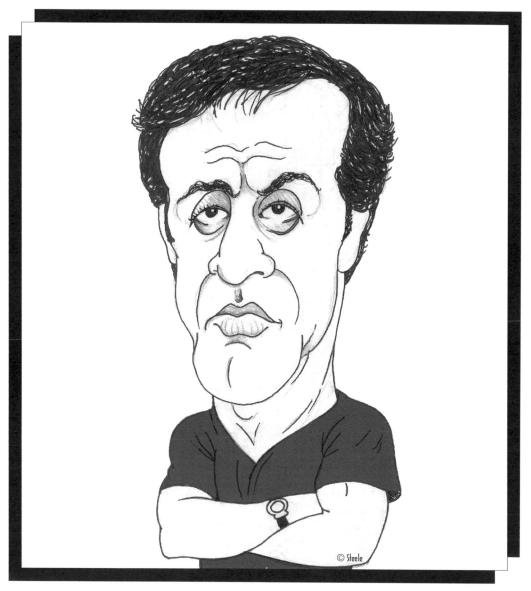

© Steele

SYLVESTER STALLONE WAS EXPELLED FROM TEN SCHOOLS

39

© Nancy Polette

SYLVESTER STALLONE
1946-

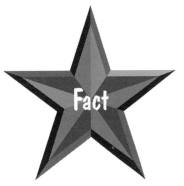

Fact

The little boy was born with
damage to a nerve in his face.
His eye was crooked.
His lower lip drooped.
When he began to speak, he was hard
to understand.
His speech was slurred.
When he went to school, other children made fun of him.
He protected himself by becoming a fighter.
His name was Sylvester Stallone.

Until he was five years old Sylvester (or Sly as he likes to be called) lived in one foster home after another. When he finally went to live with his parents, they divorced and Sly lived for a time with his mother and stepfather.

The boy was not a good student and was ever ready to punch anyone who gave him trouble. There was a lot of trouble. There were many punches. They expelled Sly from ten different schools.

Despite these troubled beginnings Sly got a scholarship to the American College in Switzerland. He took acting classes and after a successful role in *Death of A Salesman* knew that acting was what he wanted to do. He headed for Broadway where they turned him down for parts time after time because of his speech. He decided to write a script that would work for him. Its title was *Rocky.* Hollywood produced the script with Sly in the lead. It was a hit!

© Steele

Following the success of the *Rocky* films, Sly created a new character, *Rambo*. The *Rambo* films were equally successful. Sly had found a positive way to use his skills as a fighter. Rocky was the underdog who was not expected to win but fought the odds to success. Rambo used his fighting skills to defeat evil forces. Could both action heroes really be Sylvester Stallone? What do you think?

FACT OR FICTION?

OPRAH WINFREY WOWED HER BOSSES AS A TV REPORTER

OPRAH WINFREY
1954-

Oprah wowed her grandmother who heard her reading at the age of three.

Oprah wowed the congregation when she read the Bible and recited in church.

Oprah wowed her teacher with her bright mind that got her a scholarship to a better school.

Oprah wowed the judges who crowned her Miss Fire Prevention in Nashville at age seventeen.

Oprah DID NOT WOW her bosses at the TV station in Maryland where she took a job as news anchor.

"Oprah," they might have said. "You have a soft heart. You care too much. A TV news anchor can't cry at sad stories, and you do it all the time. You have to be detached. You have to report the news, not dramatize it."

Oprah could not stop laughing when something was funny. She could not hold back the tears at sad stories. Oprah cared too much.

SO . . . they gave her a television job on an early morning talk show. Here laughing and crying with her guests was fine. Here showing that she cared was fine. She has been laughing and crying and caring ever since on *The Oprah Winfrey Show*. Her fans hope that she will continue to do so for many years to come.

FACT OR FICTION?

1st Comic Book

© Steele

ALEXANDER GRAHAM BELL INVENTED
THE COMIC BOOK

ALEXANDER GRAHAM BELL
1847-1922

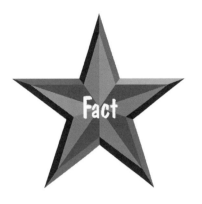
Fact

Wait a minute! Didn't Bell invent the telephone?
The telephone is what we remember Alexander Graham Bell for, but he really did invent the comic book.

Alexander was born and educated in Scotland where he graduated from high school at age thirteen. His father was a teacher of the deaf, and Alexander became his father's assistant. In the 1870's the family decided to move to Canada. Alexander got a job teaching the deaf at the Sarah Fuller School. When a child did not understand something, Alexander would draw a series of pictures. Later he got an artist to draw the pictures for him. Using his comic strip method, Alexander was successful in teaching deaf children who had learned very little in previous years.

Sound had always fascinated Alexander. He played with it. He experimented with it. Bell discovered that if he played a chord on a piano in one room that the same strings would vibrate to produce the sound on a piano in another room. Sound could be sent from one place and received in another!

While Alexander had a good mind, he was not very good with his hands. If she needed a handyman, his wife knew not to depend on

Alexander! Fortunately, he teamed up with a young mechanic named Thomas Watson who was able to put together the machine that Alexander dreamed up in his head. Eventually that machine became the telephone.

While the whole world is grateful for Bell's invention of the telephone, the world's children should be equally grateful for the comic book!

FACT OR FICTION?

THOMAS EDISON WAS FIRST IN HIS HIGH SCHOOL GRADUATING CLASS

THOMAS EDISON
1847-1931

Fiction

Young Tom had only five years of schooling and that was off and on. He did not attend high school at all.

Picture a small boy with hearing problems. The schoolroom was crowded. The room was hot. The teacher talked and talked and talked. The children were supposed to remember what the teacher said. Tom did not hear what the teacher said. His bright young mind left the school room even if his body did not. His teachers said he was dull. He was a dreamer. He did not pay attention. Edison could not learn.

Oh, how wrong they were! Tom paid close attention to anything that interested his young mind. He loved to read and taught himself from books. When he was ten, he set up a basement laboratory at home, but his experiments smelled so bad that his mother told him it had to go.

At age twelve Tom got a job as a trainboy and used one of the cars to put out a newspaper. He also used part of the car as a moving laboratory, but when his laboratory exploded and the car caught fire Tom had to cease his experiments.

To support himself Tom worked as a telegrapher but never gave up experimenting. When he was twenty-nine, he borrowed money to set up a real laboratory. Three years later the result of his experiments was the electric light! Tom Edison had taught himself more than any school ever could.

© Steele

FACT OR FICTION?

ALBERT EINSTEIN FAILED THE ENTRANCE EXAM TO ENGINEERING SCHOOL

ALBERT EINSTEIN
1879-1955

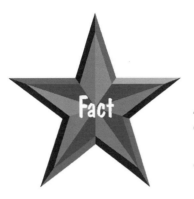

Fact

Albert Einstein did not speak until the age of four.
His speech was difficult to understand at the age of nine.
He loved fantasy.
He hated memorizing facts.
His teachers thought him dull.
At age eighteen he failed the entrance exam to engineering school.

BUT . . .

Albert Einstein became one of the world's greatest thinkers.
"What is it like to be so smart?" people would ask him.
"I have no particular talent," he said, "It's just that I stay with problems longer."

Einstein wasn't very good at taking tests. Facts bored him. He disliked the high school he attended since success depended on memorizing facts rather than searching for what was not known. Because school so bored him, his grades were not outstanding except in mathematics.

Einstein left school in Germany at the age of fifteen and at age eighteen they rejected him for engineering school because "he showed no talent." He read anything and everything that interested him and finally

completed his education in Switzerland with four years of physics and mathematics. He tried to find a teaching job, but no one would hire him, so he went to work in the Swiss Patent Office. During this time he earned a doctorate from the University of Zurich.

Important publications followed including his *Theory of Relativity*. Einstein believed in fantasy which meant more to him than any facts. "Why spend time learning facts," he said, "when we already know the answers!"

FACT OR FICTION?

© Steele

HENRY FORD INVENTED THE AUTOMOBILE

HENRY FORD
1863-1947

Fiction

In 1905 there were fifty companies in the United States trying to manufacture automobiles. Ford Motor Company was one of these. The people who put up the money for Ford's company thought he should make automobiles only for the rich. Ford had other ideas. He thought the workers who made the automobiles should be able to own them.

People laughed at Ford's idea. How could a working man possibly buy something as expensive as an automobile? Ford's answer was, "Make it less expensive."

While Ford did not invent the automobile, he DID invent the assembly line. When they put cars together one at a time, the cost of buying one was enormous. Ford came up with the idea of having a moving belt in his factory so that workers could put the cars together one piece at a time. Each worker had one special task that he did very well. Not only did this make for a quality car, but they could produce more cars faster.

Henry Ford's Model T rolled off the assembly line in 1908, and the first cars sold for $850. Seven years later Ford's assembly line was working so well that the automobile sold for $290. The working men could afford to buy the cars they made!

© Steele

While it is true that Henry Ford did not invent the automobile, he did invent a way to make it possible to own one even if you weren't rich!

FACT OR FICTION?

BILL GATES WAS A COLLEGE DROPOUT

© Nancy Polette

BILL GATES
1955-

Fact

His nickname might have been Rockabye Bill since the boy rocked back and forth when he was deep in thought. The deeper the thought, the more the rocking. Bill Gates did a lot of rocking at school because he was just plain bored. Learning was easy for Bill, and when the teacher explained subject matter he already knew, Bill turned off the teacher's voice and rocked and thought.

Bill's parents knew school bored him, and he was not doing as well as he could. They enrolled him in a private school, and it was there that Bill's love affair with the computer began. He was twelve years old, and it took only a few days before Bill knew more than the computer teacher. He mastered BASIC programming language very quickly and began writing his own programs. In his teens Bill haunted any place that had a computer. With a friend he started a small computer company to count the city traffic. It wasn't successful, but Bill predicted that that small company was only the beginning of his life with computers. "By age thirty," he said, "I will be a millionaire."

After high school Bill went to Harvard University, but Rockabye Bill was bored there, too. He went beyond his studies to develop a programming language for the first microcomputer. At age twenty he started the company Microsoft® that was to change forever the relationship of people to computers. Bill's dream was to

$$ Bill $$
$$ Gates $$

© Steele

put a computer in every home. In 1975 this seemed a ridiculous idea. Bill continued to develop software to make personal computers easy, inexpensive and enjoyable. He was so successful that he left Harvard in his junior year to devote full time to his company.

Bill was right when he predicted that one day computers would be a part of everyday life. He was only wrong about one thing. By age 30 Bill Gates had not become a millionaire, he had become a billionaire.

© Nancy Polette

FACT OR FICTION?

LOUIS PASTEUR WAS AN "A" STUDENT IN SCIENCE

LOUIS PASTEUR
1822-1895

Fiction

The father looked at his son and shook his head. "How can you become a university professor with grades like this?" he asked. "Average, average, average! My son must be more than average!"

The little boy stared at the floor. He did not want to make his father angry. But how to improve his grades was another thing. Louis had to think about the lessons the teacher presented. Sometimes he thought so long and so hard that his work was never finished. While thinking, he would often draw. The drawings were so good that it seemed becoming an artist was in his future.

His father's dream that Louis would become a teacher was not to be put aside. When Louis took the entrance exam for the Ecole Normale, the next step on his journey to greatness, he ranked twenty-four out of thirty-two applicants. They accepted Pasteur, however, and it was at the University that he began his scientific studies that led to his research on germs.

Through his research he showed that microbes too small to be seen can spread disease. He encouraged hospitals to use cleanliness to keep diseases from spreading.

He discovered that a weak form of a disease-carrying microbe can prevent disease.

He developed a vaccine against rabies. He showed how milk can be kept germ free by a heating process.

Pasteur's work with microbes was the base from which many future scientific discoveries would come. The little boy who had to think long and hard about his lessons became known as the "Father of Microbiology."

FACT OR FICTION?

NEITHER ORVILLE NOR WILBUR WRIGHT FINISHED HIGH SCHOOL

ORVILLE WRIGHT 1871-1948
WILBUR WRIGHT 1867-1912

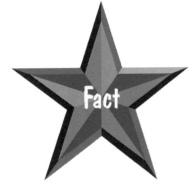

Fact

One day Bishop Wright, who was pastor of the local church, brought a present home to his two sons Orville and Wilbur. Little was he to know what would happen as a result of that present!

The present was a small helicopter-type toy that flew with the aid of rubber bands. It fascinated the boys.

While the boys were delighted with the helicopter, they were less than delighted with their studies at school. In fact, they expelled Orville from the sixth grade because his behavior was impossible. Neither boy went to high school.

While the brothers may not have been academic stars, both were good with their hands. As young men they earned their livings by making and repairing bicycles. But neither forgot the toy that flew. In 1900 Wilbur wrote:

"For some years I have been afflicted with the belief that flight is possible to man. My disease has increased with severity and I feel it will soon cost me an increased amount of money if not my life."

I wish we would have finished high school.

© Steele

Three years later, after putting together a flying machine in a barn, the brothers' dream came true. On December 17, 1903, near Kitty Hawk, North Carolina, the brothers made the first powered flight carrying a person. Each made two flights. Orville flew 120 feet in twelve seconds. Wilbur flew 852 feet in fifty-nine seconds.

Imagine what the brothers would say if told that airplanes today can fly all the way around the world without stopping!

FACT OR FICTION?

LAST in the CLASS

WINSTON CHURCHILL WAS LAST IN HIS CLASS

WINSTON CHURCHILL
1874-1965

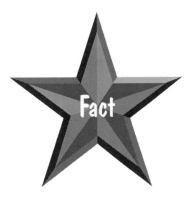

12 July 1888

Dear Lady Randolph Churchill,

Your son's "forgetfulness, carelessness, unpunctuality, and irregularity in every way have been so serious that I write to ask you to speak very gravely to him . . . "

(Signed)

Assistant Master
Henry Davidson
Harrow On the Hill

Imagine what happened to young Winston Churchill when his mother received this letter. Probably not much, since his parents were used to Winston's poor performance at school.

A few years earlier at Ascot School he was last in his class and got very "feeble" marks in composition, spelling and writing. It seemed no one could do anything to get Winston to pay attention to his lessons.

While no one would have labeled Winston Churchill gifted as a student, the world remembers him as the gifted Prime Minister who led Great Britain through its darkest hours in World War II.

Did he learn to read, write and spell? Yes! In fact he learned his lessons so well that in 1953 he won the Nobel Prize for Literature!

58

FACT OR FICTION?

© Steele

JOHN F. KENNEDY WON THE ELECTION FOR CLASS PRESIDENT AT HARVARD

JOHN F. KENNEDY
1917-1963

Fiction

John's brother Joe was best at everything he did. Joe starred in varsity football at Harvard. Joe was an honor student in his studies. Joe won nearly every campus office for which he ran. Competing with Joe was hard but John tried.

The Kennedy family had always gone to Harvard University, but when it was time for college, John chose another school. He wanted to be known for himself and not as Joe's brother. After one year, John did enter Harvard. He tried his best to compete. He made the second string football team, but a back injury stopped football forever.

Swimming was his best sport, but on the day of the competition for a place on the swimming team, John had the flu. This did not stop him from showing up and giving it his best, but he did not make a place on the team.

Since sports was not a place where John could excel, he ran against thirty-three other candidates for President of his freshman class. He was badly beaten.

Then World War II erupted, and the boy who couldn't compete showed what he could do when the going got rough. When his PT boat was destroyed, John, with great courage saved his men. The story is told in John's book, *Profiles in Courage*, for which he won the Pulitzer Prize.

© Steele

Following the War he ran for Congress and served three terms before winning the election as Senator from his state. John F. Kennedy then became the youngest man ever elected President of the United States who, with courage and determination, brought a new spirit to the American people . . . The New Frontier.

FACT OR FICTION?

Private Abe

© Steele

**ABRAHAM LINCOLN WENT INTO THE ARMY
AS A CAPTAIN AND CAME OUT AS A PRIVATE**

ABRAHAM LINCOLN
1809-1865

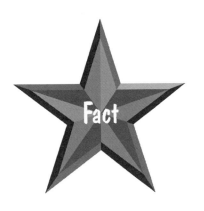

Broken treaties!

Indian uprisings!

Fearful settlers!

The year was 1832. Chief Black Hawk , the war chief of the Sacs, was determined to reclaim the lands taken by the settlers. The governor of Illinois sent out a call for militia men to fight the Indians. Abraham Lincoln was one of the first to volunteer.

They told the men of Lincoln's Company to choose their leader. They chose Lincoln who became their Captain. The sharpshooter company was ready to fight. Day after day they waited for orders. Day after day no orders came. The men had families at home and farms to run. Finally, they disbanded and went home.

Lincoln did not go home. The same day he was mustered out of the Militia he joined up again, this time as a private in the scouting service, sometimes called the Independent Spy Battalion.

No one today remembers Abraham Lincoln as a spy. Even Private Lincoln serving his country in 1832 would have had a hard time imagining that he would again serve his country as President of the United States!

FACT OR FICTION?

GENERAL GEORGE PATTON DID NOT READ UNTIL THE AGE OF TWELVE

GENERAL GEORGE PATTON
1885-1945

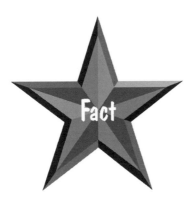

Fact

At age six he listened to his father
read about Greek heroes. He wanted to
be a Greek hero.
. . . But he couldn't read.
At age eight he could recite lines from
Homer's *Iliad and Odyssey*. He wanted to be
like Hercules.
. . . But he couldn't read.

At age ten he listened to John Mosby tell stories of his Civil War
adventures. He wanted to have adventures like that.
. . . But he couldn't read.

At age twelve he wanted to be a combat general.
. . . He knew he had to learn to read, and he did!

George Patton never lost sight of his goal to be a general. He
attended Virginia Military Institute and graduated from West Point. While he
was not at the top of his class, he showed outstanding military skills. When
World War I was raging Patton requested and got combat duty. He
became the leader of U.S. Tank Forces pushing far ahead into enemy
territory.

© Steele

When World War II exploded, Patton was
promoted to General and put in command of the
2nd Armored Division that became one of the
most effective fighting forces of the war.

The boy who couldn't read until he was
twelve, and who never learned to spell, achieved
his dream. We will always remember General
George Patton as one of the most effective
officers ever to serve his country.

Gifted or Goof Off?

© John Steele

© Nancy Polette

Gifted or Goof Off?

© John Steele

Gifted or Goof Off?

© John Steele

67

© Nancy Polette

For More Information . . .

Hans Christian Andersen
Burch, Joann. A Story About Hans Christian Andersen. Carolrhoda, 1994.
Collin, Hedwig. Young Hans Christian Andersen. Viking, 1955.
Encarta, 1994. "Andersen, Hans Christian."

Roald Dahl
Dahl, Roald. Boy: Tales of Childhood. Farrar, 1984.
Dahl, Roald. Going Solo. Farrar, 1986.
Treglown, Jeremy, Roald Dahl: A Biography. 1994.

Charles Dickens
Kaplan, Fred. Dickens, A Biography. Morrow, 1988.
Watts, Alan. Life and Times of Charles Dickens. Gramercy, 1991.

Theodore Geisel (Dr. Seuss)
Dean, Tanya. Theodore Geisel, Chelsea House, 2002.
Morgan, Judith and Neil. Dr. Seuss & Mr. Geisel: A Biography.
Weidt, Maryann. Oh, The Places He Went: A Story About Dr. Seuss.

Lucille Ball
Brady, Kathleen. Lucille, the Life of Lucille Ball. Hyperion, 1994.
Brochu, Jim. Lucy in the Afternoon. Morrow, 1990.
Higham, Charles. Lucy: The Life of Lucille Ball. St. Martins Press, 1986.

Jim Carrey
Knelman, M. Jim Carrey: The Joker is Wild. Firefly Books, 2000.
Trakin, Roy. Jim Carrey: Unmasked! SMP, 1995.

Cher
Bego, Mark. Cher If You Believe. Cooper Square Press, 2001.
Bono, Sonny. The Beat Goes On. Pocket Books, 1991.
Taraborrelli, J. Randy. Cher: A Biography. St. Martins Press, 1992.

Tom Cruise
Clarkson, Wensley. Tom Cruise: Unauthorized. Midpoint Trade Books. 1998..
Eichhorn, Dennis. Cruise. Turman, 1987.
Sanello, Frank. Cruise: The Unauthorized Biography. Taylor Pub. 1995.

Walt Disney
DiFranco, JoAnn. Walt Disney: When Dreams Come True. Dillon, 1985.
Eliot, Marc. Walt Disney: Hollywood's Dark Prince. Carol Publishing Group, 1993.

Clint Eastwood
Johnstone, Iain. The Man With No Name: A Biography of Clint Eastwood. Morrow Quill, 1981.
Schickel, Richard. Clint Eastwood: A Biography. Knopf, 1996.
Thompson, Douglas. Clint Eastwood: Riding High. Contemporary Books, 1996.

Harrison Ford
Clinch, Minty. _Harrison Ford: A Biography._ Hodder & Stoughton. 1988..
Jenkins, Gary. _Harrison Ford: Imperfect Hero._ Carol Publishing Group, 1998.

George Gershwin
Armitage, Merle. _George Gershwin Man and Legend._ Ayer Co. Pub. 1958.
Ewen, David. _George Gershwin, His Journey of Greatness._ Prentice Hall, 1970.

Whoopi Goldberg
Adams, Mary Agnes. _Whoopi Goldberg: From Street to Stardom._ Dillon, 1996.
Blue, Rose. _Whoopi Goldberg._ Chelsea House, 1995.
Caper, William. _Whoopi Goldberg: Comedian and Movie Star._ Enslow, 1999.

James Earl Jones
Jones, James Earl. _Voices and Silences._ Scribner, 1993.
Hasday, Judy. _James Earl Jones._ Chelsea House, 2000.

Michael Jordan
Beahm, Geoge. _Michael Jordan: A Shooting Star._ McMeel, 1994.
Clary, Jack. _Michael Jordan._ Smithmark, 1992.
Dolan, Sean. _Michael Jordan._ Chelsea House, 1993.

Elvis Presley
Guralnick, Peter. _Last Train to Memphis: The Rise of Elvis Presley._ Little Brown, 1994.
Daily, Robert. _Elvis Presley: The King of Rock 'N' Roll._ Watts, 1996.

Steven Spielberg
Baxter, John. _Steven Spielberg: The Unauthorized Biography._ HarperCollins, 1996.
Sanello, Frank. _Spielberg, The Man, The Movies, The Mythology._ Taylor, 1996.
Mabery, D.L. _Steven Spielberg._ Lerner, 1986.

Sylvester Stallone
Eichhorn, Dennis. _Stallone._ Turman, 1986.
Gross, Edward. _Rocky and the Films of Sylvester Stallone._ Pioneer, 1990.

Oprah Winfrey
Bly, Nellie. _Oprah! Up Close and Down Home._ Kensington, 1993.
King, Norman. _Everybody Loves Oprah! Her Remarkable Life Story._ Morrow, 1987.
Mair, George. _Oprah Winfrey: The Real Story._ Wheeler Publishing, 1995.

Alexander Graham Bell
Bruce, Robert. _Alexander Graham Bell and the Conquest of Solitude._ Little, 1973.
Davidson, Margaret. _Story of Alexander Graham Bell._ Dell, 1997.

Thomas Edison
Bolton, Sarah. _Famous Men of Science._ Crowell, 1960.
Greene, Carol. _Thomas Alva Edison: Bringer of Light._ Children's Press, 1985.
Clark, Ronald. _Edison: The Man Who Made the Future._ Putnams, 1977.

Albert Einstein
Clark, Ronald. <u>Einstein: The Life and Times.</u> Crowell, 1971.
Ireland, Karin. <u>Albert Einstein</u>. Silver Burdett, 1989.
McPherson, Stephanie. <u>Ordinary Genius: The Story of Albert Einstein.</u> Carolrhoda, 1995.

Henry Ford
Kent, Zachary. <u>Story of Henry Ford and the Automobile.</u> Children's Press, 1990.
Middleton, Haydn. <u>Henry Ford: The People's Carmaker.</u> Carolrhoda, 1995.

Bill Gates
Dickinson, Joan. <u>Bill Gates: Billionaire Computer Genius</u>. Enslow, 1997.
Forman, Michael. <u>Bill Gates: Software Billionaire.</u> Cestwood House, 1999.
Simon, Charnan. <u>Bill Gates: Helping People Use Computers.</u> Children's Press, 1997.

Louis Pasteur
Birch, Beverly. <u>Louis Pasteur.</u> Gareth Stevens, 1989.
Benz, Francis. <u>Pasteur: Knight of the Laboratory</u>. Dodd Mead, 1938.

Wright Brothers
Crouch, Tom. <u>The Bishop's Boys: A Life of Wilbur & Orville Wright</u>. Norton, 1989.
Franchere, Ruth. <u>Wright Brothers</u>. Crowell, 1972.

Winston Churchill
Schneider, Robert. <u>Novelist to a Generation: The Life and Thoughts of Winston Churchill.</u> Bowling Green University Press, 1976.
Titus, Warren. <u>Winston Churchill.</u> Crowell, 1972.

John F. Kennedy
Hamilton, Nigel. <u>JFK: Reckless Youth</u>. Random House, 1992.
Levine, I.E. <u>John Kennedy: Young Man in the White House.</u> Messner, 1964.

Abraham Lincoln
Dupuy, Trevor. <u>The Military Life of Abraham Lincoln, Commander in Chief.</u> Watts, 1969.
Marrin, Albert. <u>Commander-in-Chief, Abraham Lincoln.</u> Dutton, 1997.

George S. Patton
Blumenson, Martin. <u>Patton: The Man Beneath the Legend.</u> Morrow, 1985.
Devaney, John. <u>"Blood and Guts:" The True Story of General George S. Patton, U.S.A.</u> Messner, 1982.